DECOLONISING THE ACADEMY
A CASE FOR CONVIVIAL SCHOLARSHIP

Francis B. Nyamnjoh

DECOLONISING THE ACADEMY
A CASE FOR CONVIVIAL SCHOLARSHIP

Carl Schlettwein Lecture 14
Basler Afrika Bibliographien

© 2020 The authors
© 2020 Basler Afrika Bibliographien
Basler Afrika Bibliographien
Namibia Resource Centre & Southern Africa Library
Klosterberg 23
P. O. Box
CH 4051 Basel
Switzerland
www.baslerafrika.ch

CARL SCHLETTWEIN
STIFTUNG

The Basler Afrika Bibliographien is part of the Carl Schlettwein Foundation

Cover image: Removal of the Rhodes statue situated on the campus
of the University of Cape Town on 9 April 2015 (picture: Michael
Hammond und Roger Sedres, University of Cape Town)
Editors: Veit Arlt, Cassandra Mark-Thiesen, Oluwasooto Ajayi
Layout and typesetting: Tilo Richter
ISBN 978-3-906927-25-1
ISSN 2297–7058

FOREWORD

The Carl Schlettwein Lecture 2019 coincided with the conference *Africa and the Academy in the 21st Century,* taking place between 1 and 2 November 2019. Hosted at the University of Basel in cooperation between the Swiss Society for African Studies and the Centre for African Studies Basel, this interactive and interdisciplinary conference drew in scholars from across Switzerland and different parts of Europe and Africa to discuss the past, present and future of African Studies and its related disciplines. This occasion represented the perfect backdrop for the distinguished lecture by Francis Nyamnjoh, Professor of Social Anthropology at the University of Cape Town.

In an essay titled *Academic Whispers,* the great American writer Toni Morrison recalls her experience in the 1980s of colleagues and students struggling to come to agreement on what she calls "the true purpose of the discourse" (Morrison, 2019, p. 198), in her case referring to the discourse within the field of study of African-American literature. What she described as a whispered dialogue was only exacerbated by overt attacks from without; as outsiders questioned what right this field had to exist in the first place. Her words reflected the multiple planes of discourse at the forefront of the conference; one line of inquiry produced questions concerning how those conducting studies of Africa could defend or rather give further legitimacy to African Studies and its related disciplines in the broader academic community. A second line of inquiry, pursued with much greater vigor over the two days of the conference, included discussions between the speakers and members of the audience over how to enhance the field from within moving forward and especially in connection to ongoing "decolonising" debates.

As Morrison reminds the reader towards the end of her essay, these debates are not (or, rather, ought not to be regarded as) confined to any particular discipline or university. In actuality, they are about the value that we give to education, science, and intellectual freedom (p. 204). Working from a similar perspective, in his most recent work, Nyamnjoh reminds his readers of the great intellectual riches and possibilities awaiting us on the other side of academic "decolonisation".

Although Francis Nyamnjoh is known for his broad scholarship embedded in all facets of everyday life, the student movements in South Africa in 2016, which found reverberations at universities in other parts of the world, have clearly been one of his most recent preoccupations. Nevertheless, he neither tackles them in a way that restricts this crisis to South Africa (or Africa for that matter), nor in a way that limits the resulting challenges to higher education alone. His concern is broader. In mapping out one possible academic future, his appeal is for convivial processes of knowledge production, not to forget the scholarly community to match—one that is flexible, inclusive, and, yes, consciously incomplete. Francis Nyamnjoh's words serve as an important guiding light in these times of change.

Cassandra Mark-Thiesen
Basel, 3 December 2019

DECOLONISING THE ACADEMY
A CASE FOR CONVIVIAL SCHOLARSHIP

SETTING THE SCENE:
KNOWLEDGE AND GLOBAL POWER

I recently read *Knowledge and Global Power: Making New Sciences in the South* (Collyer, Connell, Maia, & Morell, 2019). I find this book very relevant in contemplating Africa and the academy in the 21st century. It explores the relationship between knowledge and global power. The authors Fran Collyer, Raewyn Connell, João Maia and Robert Morrell discuss, among other issues, global hegemony in the economy of knowledge and alternative possibilities. Global knowledge production, they argue, is still dominated by the Global North. Instructive to my interest in convivial scholarship, the authors bring to the study their various backgrounds, their life experiences in Africa, Australia, and Latin America, and their skills in historical, sociological, archival, and qualitative and quantitative research methods. Data on knowledge producers in selected fields was collected mainly via semi-structured interviews (on careers, everyday work routines, networks, and sources of information). This included interviewing publishers. Other sources of data included the Web of Science website, which was consulted to establish the competitiveness of the three case study countries. The three countries, all in the Global South, were among the top 25 countries globally in 2015, despite the fact that the Web of Science is biased in favour of the Global North. This speaks to the potential for creative innovation in the making of new sciences, for example when new fields of inquiry emerge that challenge established disciplinary or conceptual repertoires and logics of practice.

The study confirms predictable continuities and draws attention to the making of new sciences in the Global South, with South Africa, Brazil and Australia as case studies. Specifically, it considers knowledge production on HIV/AIDS, climate change, and gender issues, which fields of study are multidisciplinary in nature and bring into conversation the physical and biomedical sciences, humanities, and social sciences. The authors argue that inequalities and power relations in the production and circulation of knowledge are dynamic and shaped in part by histories of encounter and struggle. The global knowledge system is dynamic, imperfectly integrated, and characterised by tensions stemming from issues such as language, rhythms of workforce creation, and intellectual and conceptual problems (Collyer et al., 2019, pp. 154–155).

Though Eurocentric knowledge canons predominate and continue to create and animate relations of dependency in the Global South, which is still very much peripheral in the global knowledge economy, work in new domains of study, such as HIV/AIDS, climate change and gender, has created "more room for Southern researchers to use their expertise and location to swing the pendulum away from Northern dominance and towards more equal terms of engagement" (p. 52). The dynamism in knowledge production is evident in the increased productivity of Southern researchers and the accommodation of their Northern counterparts. However modestly, "Southern researchers have ensured Southern visibility" (p. 53) in current and future discussions in the three domains of research highlighted in the book.

The study discusses scholarly publishing and how the Global North is favoured by a focus on journals, which are of major Northern publishing houses and preponderantly in English. Emphasising journal articles when assessing academic performance "tends to underplay the knowledge production of disciplines that place greater or equal importance on books, policy reports, newspapers, and other products including creative works and performances" (p. 88). Such lop-sidedness works in favour of the physical, biomedical and technological sciences and to the detriment of the humanities, social sciences and arts.

CREATIVELY COPING WITH EXTRAVERSION AND INEQUALITIES

The study speaks to Paulin Hountondji's idea of extraversion (1997)—a structural condition that sustains the adoption of frameworks and methods developed in the Global North. Such practices perpetuate unfavourable terms of engagement for the Global South, skewing relations and perspectives in favour of the Global North. The authors recognise that "knowledge workers in both the North and the South are situated in an international division of labour which concentrates prestige, resources, and the sources for publishing in the Global North" (Collyer et al. 2019, p. 81). Though extraversion is the dominant mode of knowledge production in the three countries studied, a careful analysis of the everyday practices of intellectual knowledge workers in the

Global South points to how they develop creative strategies "to cope with the unequal distribution of resources, prestige and wealth" (p. 54). The investigation into knowledge production practices considered intellectual tools (such as email, software programmes, and technological hardware), labour routines, research skills, global research networks, and the challenges of writing.

The authors go beyond simply describing how the Global South mimics the Global North in knowledge production to explore "the very complex (and sometimes contradictory) process in which knowledge workers actively deal with subordination" (p. 81). The relationships are far from being ones of passive dependency or uncontested domination. Southern knowledge producers are active and ever more creative and strategic in navigating and negotiating the challenges of subordination. The book is thus as much about empirically substantiating the reality of extraversion, in the classical sense, as it is about evidencing how knowledge producers of the Global South, through innovative coping and transformation strategies, grapple with the contradictions and difficulties in the global knowledge economy (p. 146).

The study reiterates that context—whether geographical, socioeconomic, political or cultural—matters in knowledge production. Thus, actions to mitigate hegemony might include "the creation of local research programmes, the founding of research centres, and the linking of research to public policy addressing local problems in distinctive ways" (p. 166). The book reveals how knowledge workers and knowledge-based organisations react to the global hegemony of knowledge producers located in the Global North. To the authors, no one can escape the global hegemony of the North in knowledge production and circulation. At the same time, "a hegemonic situation does not simply mean domination, nor does it imply passivity" (p. 146). Some scholars in the Global South accept the hegemony completely, some resist it strongly, and many make complex compromises.

FROM IMPERIAL SCIENCE
TO RESPECTFUL RELATIONS

Imperial science (Ake, 2012[1997]; Comaroff & Comaroff, 2010[1991])—a term the authors find much more accurate than the label "Western Science" (Collyer et al., 2019, p. 9)—from the European centre met up with epistemic orders at colonial peripheries. European powers tried to obliterate, appropriate, or, in some instances, recognise and even honour the competing local knowledges and peripheral epistemes (p. 12). "Except where colonisation involved absolute genocide, elements of pre-colonisation knowledge have survived" (p. 13). In light of the growing clamour by indigenous knowledge movements for formerly colonised people to become the subjects of their own knowledge projects and educational practices, the authors propose what they term as "mosaic epistemology" and argue that it offers "a clear alternative to Northern hegemony and global inequality, replacing the priority of one knowledge system with respectful relations among many" (ibid.). This is not to imply, however, argue the authors, that a mosaic epistemology is devoid of pitfalls, especially considering and factoring in the perpetual dynamism of cultures and societies.

MAKING INTERCONNECTIONS AND
PRIORITIZING INTERDEPENDENCIES

I privilege interconnections and interdependencies that nourish and celebrate scholarship of conviviality grounded in incompleteness. As used here, incompleteness is not an inadequacy to feel inferior about, but rather, a norm to recognise and provide for in our actions and interactions with fellow humans, and with the world out there, both real and imagined. In a spirit of interconnections, I would like to reach out to two ancestors of thinking and writing Africa, Amos Tutuola on the idea of incompleteness, and Chinua Achebe, on the importance of mobility. I refer to them to invite complex and nuanced conversations on Africa and the academy in the 21st century. I assume, like Amos Tutuola did in *The Palm-Wine Drinkard, My Life in the Bush of Ghosts* (Tutuola, 1952 & 1954) and his other writings, that Africa and being African, like every other part of and every other being in the world, is incomplete and always in need of relationships with others (beings, things, ideas) to extend themselves in the interest of greater efficacy in their aspirations to produce, reproduce and improve upon their sense of being and becoming. How can one provide for interconnections and incompleteness without recognising debt and indebtedness to others—beings, things and ideas? Without incompleteness, how is one to do justice to the study of Africa and Africans as dynamic realities in a world constantly on the move?

I find it compelling to think with proverbs and metaphors. Let me share a proverb with which many of you are already familiar, from Chinua Achebe's novel *Arrow of God*: "The world is like a mask dancing. If you want to see it well you do not stand in one place" (1974[1964], p. 46.) Permit me to adapt it slightly as follows: "*Africa is like a mask dancing. If you want to see it well you do not stand in one place.*" Let's continue to explore: "*Africans are like masks dancing. If you want to see them well you do not stand in one place.*" Nimble-footed realities require nimble-footed intellects and nimble-footed scholarship. Nimble-footed intellects need to bring historical ethnography into conversation with the ethnographic present. They need to draw on and distil from yesterday and today to inform a far-from-linear future. Let's draw on and adapt Achebe yet again: "*Disciplines are like masks dancing. If you want to see them well you do not stand in one place.*"

Everything moves—people, things and ideas—in predictable and unpredictable ways. It should not surprise us that Africa moves and has always moved. If the deep historical conviction that Africa is the cradle of human kind holds,[1] then everyone, regardless of their present location in the world, is African to a lesser or greater degree. The circulation of things, ideas and people is not the monopoly of any particular group, community or society. Mobility and circulation lead to encounters of various forms, encounters that are (re)defining in myriad ways. If people, their things and their ideas circulate, it follows that their identities, personal or collective, move as well. Through encounters with others, mobile people are constantly navigating, negotiating, accommodating or rejecting difference (in things, ideas, practices and relations) in an open-ended manner that makes of them permanent works in progress. Put differently, and seen through the prism of histories of mobility, personal or collective, identities (even when claimed exclusively and in the singular) are always composite and open-ended. No mobility or interaction, whether horizontal, vertical, or circular in nature, leaves anyone, anything or any idea indifferent, even if it does not always result in immediate, palpable or tangible change. No encounter results in uncontested domination or total passivity. Some people may wilt in the face of domination, some resist it fervently, and others navigate and negotiate the tensions and contradictions brought about by the reality of domination in complex, creative and innovative ways. Such creative and oftentimes circuitous navigation may hold potential for new and more convivial forms of identity, practice and relating. In terms of the disciplines and the place of African voices in the study of Africa therein, the personal story and journeys of Emmanuel Akyeampong, a Ghanaian historian who studied in Ghana and the USA and who actively contributed to the setting up of an African studies centre at Harvard University, are particularly instructive in how they offer great food for thought on the epistemological, conceptual and methodological implications of mobilities in the making and remaking of the relationships that feed curiosities about the place of Africa in the world and the world in Africa (Akyeampong, 2012).

Revisiting debates such as the one in the 1990s of *Africa and the Disciplines*,[2] affords us the opportunity to use old questions as a springboard for exploring new ones, such as those of change and continuities in power dynamics in global knowledge production, distribution and consumption explored by Collyer, Connell, Maia and Morrell in *Knowledge and Global Power* (2019). If *Africa and the Disciplines*—which the editors targeted primarily at "those who hold power in the academy and Africanists who, by and large, do not" (Bates et al., 1993, p. xxi)—were about interrogating "the standing of African studies in the modern university" and "the impact of the research in Africa on the core disciplines" (p. xi). The writers considered the social production of knowledge, the production process and those involved, as well as the resources that make knowledge production possible. Is such work relevant to current persistent clamours for the decolonisation of knowledge production and consumption globally, and on and about Africa and Africans in particular,[3] and especially in their complexities and mobilities? How can scholars of today usefully draw on such work? African knowledge producers are increasingly aware that the predicaments of those they research, teach and publish on are not discipline-bound or confined to a particular geographical space, and that doing them justice requires, as compellingly argued by the authors of *Knowledge and Global Power*, working in teams, within institutions and in local and global networks of cooperation, as well as with stakeholders beyond the ivory tower.

Kenyan anthropologist Mwenda Ntarangwi (2019) uses the example of the social media era, in which scholars increasingly do not have the monopoly of representation, to invite anthropologists to pay greater attention to "heightened scrutiny by multiple players" facilitated by social media, without sacrificing "the nuanced analysis that only comes from long-term familiarity with place and people" (p. 442). If one is to adopt a complex and nuanced understanding of Africa and being African, steeped in histories of mobility and interconnections, how does one recognise and provide for a debate of *Africa and the Disciplines* in the 21st century that is not unduly confined to bounded and often racialised, ethnicised and gendered ideas of who qualifies to belong or not belong to particular places and spaces? How does one account for, as well as challenge the hierarchies of mobility and visibility that produce an industry of scholarship on the predicament of *Outsiders Within*—those caught betwixt and between the ever diminishing circles of inclusion and aptly described by African-American anthropologist Faye Harrison (2008)?

An investment in answering these questions would help address the admission by Bates, Mudimbe and O'Barr that, "While often failing to achieve universal knowledge, disciplines are distinguished by their commitment to that ideal (1993, xii)." A 21st century debate of *Africa and the Disciplines* should do more than target those with power in the academy in the North—non-Africanists and Africanists alike—by focusing on similar dynamics within the African continent, and among Africans in their nimble-footedness.

Current and unfolding scholarship on and around alternative theorisation inspired by experiences in and of the Global South, and that contests the traditional passivity and silencing associated with the Global South in relations with the Global North, are instructive in this regard (Connell, 2007; Santos, 2007; Ntarangwi, 2010; Comaroff & Comaroff, 2011; Harrison, 2016). Such scholarship stresses the need to emphasize that, far from resigning to disempowerment and a sense of intellectual inferiority, scholarly communities of practice in Africa and indeed the Global South are often creative and fertile grounds where competing and complementary intellectual traditions cross-fertilise one another (Harrison, 2016). Even in all that constructive creativity, processes of producing new knowledge are always incomplete and open to the possibility of new engagements, collaborations, and respective debates. Hence, as thinkers, we need to be freed from the constraints and obstacles that have engendered the hierarchies of differentially calibrating our scholarly work, often along lines of ethno-race, nation, gender, sexuality, religion, and whatever else.

Granted that disciplines and their imbued hierarchies are themselves nimble-footed and that they unsettle when settled or unsettled, how does the fact of mobile Africans and mobile disciplines reproduce, contest and reconstitute the object of study (Akyeampong, 2012)? A 21st century *Africa and the Disciplines* debate requires reflection on the history of the mobility of disciplines and how, and the extent to which, disciplines are reconstituted in new geographies according to new imperatives and in multidirectional flows. Assuming, without reification, the binary between the Global North and Global South in a centre-periphery framework, the Global North would have to recognise its incompleteness as well as its debts and indebtedness to the Global South by engaging seriously with the reconstitution and multidirectional flows of disciplines, beyond the mere fixation with superficial indicators of representation and accommodation. Instead of merely focusing on the tokenism of representation and inclusion for certain social categories (blacks, Africans, women, youth, etc.), there is an urgent imperative to engage with how such historic absences have influenced how the disciplines are constituted and interrogate what inclusion would mean for the very object of study in its dynamism and compositeness. If historically excluded Africans, in all their nimble-footedness, engage with and are engaged by mobile disciplines, how can that engagement weigh in on the object of study and instruments of particular disciplines?

What does it say of Africa, being African or of Africa decent in a world where regardless of geography, one's race and ethnicity play a major role, over and above other factors such as class, gender, sexuality and age, in the recognition and visibility that one attracts, however prestigious the institution in the Global North or Global South where one trained or practices (Harrison, 2019)? What does it tell us that Stanford-trained Faye Harrison writes of predicaments she experiences in the USA, as an African-American female anthropologist in a manner that resonates with female anthropologists in Africa (black and white alike) and also male anthropologists (black and white alike)? And what does it mean that the very same hierarchies she challenges are reproduced in Africa? If anything, this speaks to the need to factor power and politics into our quest to understand the logic and practice of knowledge production globally and to always situate such dynamics and scholarship within a framework of interconnecting local and global hierarchies (Gupta & Ferguson, 1992 & 1997). Faye Harrison is a composite being, always adding ever more complexity and nuance to her being. Clearly situated in the US context, she makes an effort to glocalise her thinking and writing and to reposition it at a transnational crossroads of conversations (Harrison, 1991), in a manner that evokes the "mosaic epistemology" suggested by the authors of *Knowledge and Global Power* (Collyer et al., 2019). Being an insider or an outsider is a layered and open-ended work in progress, permanently subject to renegotiation and best understood as relational and situational and, ultimately, as always incomplete. Interconnecting global and local hierarchies—be these informed by race, place, class, culture, gender, age or other factors—shape connections and disconnections, and produce, reproduce and contest distinctions between insiders and outsiders, which distinctions are political and ideological constructs defying empirical evidence and the messiness of lived experiences.

The traditional anthropological subject (referred to as "the native" or "the other")—(im)mobilised and seen and related to as a mobile and creative agent—seeks inclusion as a *bona fide* ethnographer with license to self-study and to study those who have traditionally studied them, often with little mastery of indigenous/endogenous/"native" languages, epistemologies and histories beyond contrived colonial frames of reference (Owusu, 2012[1978]; Phipps, 2019). What have been the challenges and successes? What does it take to be included in the inner circles of the discipline by the disciplinary instances of legitimation—those with the authority to police the borders of the anthropological tribe, distinguishing between insiders and outsiders, and maintaining real or imagined disciplinary purity? What does it take for anthropological insiders to seek or accommodate competing or complementary traditions of knowledge and meaning-making? To what extent has Anthropology entertained conversations and co-production with other disciplines and how has this been evidenced in the ethnographies produced by African anthropologists and anthropologists of Africa? How have anthropologists who have felt marginalised or misrepresented within the discipline and its traditions or practices of representation, on account for instance of their race, ethnicity, class, gender, sexuality, generation or geography, gone about contesting or seeking recognition and representation within the discipline? And with what successes? In view of postcolonial clamours for decolonisation, epistemological inclusion, and flexibility, Faye Harrison (2019), although in statutory terms an anthropologist of the Global North, articulates kindred concerns and suggests ways forward on how to produce ethnographies sensitive to the power relations and privileges overt or implicit in the relationships (visible and otherwise) which inform knowledge production and the assumptions that underpin the process.

Deep history aside, in what specifically concerns contemporary Africans in the diaspora and on the continent, we need to take seriously Faye Harrison's call—informed by her compositeness of being and status, experiences and predicaments as a female African-

American anthropologist in US anthropological circles—for the decolonisation of anthropology through:

- its rehistoricisation;
- rethinking, reworking and reassessing what constitutes theory and theorising and who is authorised to do it;
- rethinking the implications and possibilities of both intradisciplinarity and interdisciplinarity for anthropological inquiry and analysis;
- the pursuit of a socially responsible ethics and politics of ethnographic research for producing ethnography and ethnographically informed social analysis;
- mapping the mediated connections between the local and supralocal—national, regional, and "global"—spheres;
- interrogating the ways in which anthropology is organised and practised in both academic and non-academic contexts;
- its further democratisation as an intellectual community;
- mobilising knowledge and professional resources for forms of democratic engagement that link the academic pursuits of anthropologists to public interests; and
- decentring Western dominance.

(Harrisson, 2008, 37–48)

It is in its capacity to challenge a tendency towards over-
ly dichotomous categorisations and to reveal interconnections that makes Harrison's *Outsiders Within* a key
text in discussing Africa and the academy in the 21st century—beyond the narrow confines of scholarship produced in and on the bounded geography called Africa.
It is an approach I share and recommend (Nyamnjoh,
2012). Disciplinary heartlands need the rejuvenating
winds of ferment blowing from nimble-footed disciplinary practitioners facilitating at the frontiers insightful
cross-border conversations with fellow disciplines, in
the interest of understanding nuanced complexities and
the messiness of being and becoming human in a world
permanently on the move (Gupta & Ferguson, 1997).

INCOMPLETENESS AND
CONVIVIAL SCHOLARSHIP

Understanding the nimble-footedness of being African
and the unboundedness of being, becoming and belong-
ing as Africans or otherwise, this address invites us to
build on the debate on *Africa and the Disciplines* of the
early 1990s, by recognising and providing for a disposition of incompleteness that lends itself to convivial
scholarship. If it is normal to be incomplete both biologically and socially, then it is problematic to claim superiority either biologically and socially (Nyamnjoh,
2017[2015] & 2017). Recognising interdependence and
promoting collaboration enriches scholarship. For the
researcher, this means co-elaboration, co-investigation,
co-production, and co-provision for the compositeness
of being that acknowledges the outsider within and the

insider without as intimate strangers (Nyamnjoh, 2010). Recognising interdependence and conducting convivial scholarship requires making a deliberate effort to reach in, identify, contemplate, understand, embrace and become intimate with the stranger within us, in individuals and societies alike (Simmel, 1950; Lategan, 2018; Devisch, 2017). Such recognition of incompleteness and provision for the cross-fertilisation of ideas should be within and between disciplines, and between researchers/scholars/academics and those outside the academy (Nyamnjoh, 2019). We have the audacity and power to challenge and rethink knowledge production. We can promote and demand the imperatives of seeing, hearing, feeling, touching and smelling the world from different angles, different vantage points, different backgrounds, different orientations, different perspectives, and different interests, as suggested by Chinua Achebe in his proverb about the dancing mask. Imagine knowledge production as truly participatory, a process in which no race, gender, culture, ethnic or age group, geography or any other social category has a monopoly.

Recurrent clamours for universities in Africa (and indeed, elsewhere) to provide for greater inclusion (Nyamnjoh, 2016) are a reminder that, although intended as convivial spaces par excellence, universities are not as convivial in practice as one would expect. Equally unconvivial, as highlighted by the example of the continued dominance of publishing and indicators of scholarly visibility by the Global North in *Knowledge and Global Power* discussed above, are processes of knowledge production that champion delusions of superiority and zero-sum games of absolute winners and losers, much to the detriment of the ideal of education as "the refinement of human sensibilities" and promotion of "the capacity for human understanding and moral conduct" called for by Bates, Mudimbe and O'Barr in *Africa and the Disciplines* (1993, p. xiii). Notwithstanding their universalistic pretensions, disciplines tend to encourage introversion and a hierarchy of credibility that privileges extraversion in North-South relations (Hountondji, 1997; Collyer et al., 2019), and to emphasise exclusionary fundamentalisms of heartlands rather than inclusionary overtures of borderlands, frontiers and compositeness of being such as ought to be inspired by the reality of normalcy of incompleteness. Frequenting crossroads and engaging in frontier conversations is frowned upon, if not prohibited. If allowed in principle, inter- and multi- and trans-disciplinary dispositions are more claimed than practised, because scholars stick to their spots like leopards and, like porcupines won't let go of their quills.

Despite quests for distinction through science and reason, scholars are creatures of habit. Scarcity of conviviality in universities, between disciplines, and among scholars suggests that the production, positioning and consumption of knowledge are far from unbiased and disinterested processes. Knowledge production is socially and politically mediated by hierarchies of humanity (informed by but not confined to factors such as race, geography, ethnicity, class, gender, sexuality and age) and human agency stemming from relations of power. Given the resilience of colonial education in Africa and among Africans, endogenous traditions of knowledge popular across the continent, do not receive the recognition and representation they deserve. As Gloria Emeagwali and George Sefa Dei observe, even when the relevance of endogenous African knowledges is recognised, one is left "under no illusion as to the discriminatory tendencies discernible in the academy" (2014, p. xi), where a hierarchy of capital of knowledges obtains. While "some bodies of knowledge have been privileged and made dominant, other forms of knowledge are still being contested and are in the process of being delegitimized" (Ibid.). Conviviality in knowledge production entails not just seeking conversations and collaboration with and across disciplines in the conventional sense suggested by the authors of *Knowledge and Global Power,* but also, and even more importantly, the integration of sidestepped popular epistemologies informed by popular universes and ideas of reality—some of which are explored in *African Indigenous Knowledge and the Disciplines* (Emeagwali et al., 2014; Cooper& Morrell, 2014)—and which I have discussed abundantly elsewhere (Nyamnjoh, 2017, 2019).

Truly convivial scholarship does not seek, the way conventional debates on *Africa and the Disciplines* have, to define and confine. Rather than describing and limiting Africans in relation to territories, geographies, racial and ethnic categories, classes, genders, generations, religions or whatever other identity marker is in vogue, convivial scholarship should provide for the compositeness of being and becoming African as a permanent work in progress. If the call for conviviality, inclusion, multilayeredness and compositeness of being and relating is to be more than just a free for all, everything goes, hotchpotch of views and perspectives, convivial scholarship must challenge the academy to embrace and use the same critical consciousness that supposedly engendered the disciplines, their canons and their logics of practice, in contesting and transcending unproductive fixations with disciplinary boundaries and credos. Convivial scholarship confronts and humbles the challenge of over-prescription, over-standardisation and over-prediction—in short, it seeks to undo the McDonaldisation of the disciplines (Ritzer, 2019[1992]). It disrupts and subverts standardised and routinized reproduction of disciplinary structures of power and privilege, structures that scare away humility, curiosity, reflection, open-mindedness and creative renewal. It advocates for combining disciplinary depth and sharpness with open-minded critical consciousness and inclusivity in approach. It is critical and evidence-based, for example, being critical about sources and McDonaldised ideas of evidence. It is a scholarship that sees the human in the natural and the supernatural, the local in the global and the global in the local. It brings seeming disparities into informed conversations, conversations which do not ignore the hierarchies and power relations at play at both micro and macro levels of being and becoming. Convivial scholarship challenges us—however grounded we may be in our disciplines and their logics of practice—to cultivate the disposition to be present everywhere at the same time. This capacity for presence in simultaneous multiplicities is attainable and sharpened through a recognition and provision for a compositeness of being, and in the capacity of disciplinary practitioners to accommodate disciplinary outsiders as a way of affording disciplinary insiders the opportunity to spread their wings and renew their canons. It is a scholarship that cautions disciplines, their borders, and gatekeepers to open up and creatively embrace difference and dynamism. It insists on an openness to the sensitivities and sensibilities that our compositeness of being imbues in us as students of society, such that we are able to do the fullest justice to the subjectivities of the composite "others" whose sociality we seek to understand and represent in our scholarship. With convivial scholarship, there are no final answers. Only permanent questions and ever exciting new angles of questioning. Such scholarship is predicated upon recognising and providing for incompleteness as a necessary attribute of being, from persons to disciplines and traditions of knowing and knowledge making.

DISMANTLING PERIPHERIES OF A DICTATORIAL KNOWLEDGE ECONOMY

Let me conclude with *Knowledge and Global Power*, the book I started with. It provides much food for thought in relation to convivial scholarship and the need to recognise and provide for debt and indebtedness in the mobility of beings, things, and ideas. The study highlights how it is possible, through networking and complimentary strategies, to make ends meet at the peripheries of a global knowledge economy dominated by the Global North. Faye Harrison, in 2012, discussed how some African and diasporic African anthropologists and other knowledge producers do just that in navigating the "domestic and international peripheries" to which they are subjected in their intellectual endeavours and suggests how to go about dismantling such hierarchies (Harrison, 2012). The Council for the Development of Social Science Research in Africa (CODESRIA) and other knowledge production networks and scholarly associations are proof in the pudding of how African scholars negotiate recognition and representation for themselves and for traditions of knowledge production in tune with the predicaments of those they study. The activities do not always have to be mediated by gatekeepers of knowledge institutions in the Global North, even when funding comes from the Global North (Hoffmann, 2017; Hountondji, 1997).

I, by way of example, demonstrated that it is possible to publish with an African publisher and not perish, and even win a prestigious prize in the Global North. A case in point is my 2016 book *#RhodesMustFall: Nibbling at Resilient Colonialism in South Africa,* published by Langaa Research and Publishing, created in 2005 in Bamenda, Cameroon.[4] The book, which documents the 2015 student movements for decolonisation that began at the University of Cape Town and spread to other universities in South Africa and beyond—was awarded the ASAUK 2018 Fage & Oliver Prize for best monograph.[5] With the multiple possibilities of representation, visibility, dissemination, and networking availed by advances in information and communication technologies, it is no longer a given to perish simply because one is writing from or published in Africa, as used to be the case (Nyamnjoh, 2004).

Highlighting pockets of alternatives to the dominant order should by no means imply a trivialisation of the power imbalances between disciplinary centres of the Global North and peripheries of the Global South, in what Japanese anthropologist Takami Kuwayama terms "the academic world system" in his discussion of Japanese anthropology's recognition problem internationally (Kuwayama, 2017). It should be possible, however, in what concerns Africa, to have an Africa-centred approach to knowledge production that is driven neither by Eurocentrism nor Afrocentrism, but instead invites scholars, in their critical consciousness, to use whatever concepts and research tools they deem most appropriate in studying Africa and the rest of the world (Cooper & Morrell, 2014). Context, after all, does matter.

A good case in point of how context matters is provided by Mozambican anthropologist Euclides Gonçalves. He illustrates how the introduction of an anthropology Master's programme at Eduardo Mondlane University in Maputo in 2015—a context in which many a professional anthropologist is driven to seek consultancies with NGOs in order to make ends meet—was determined far less by considerations for disciplinary canons, than by the need to tailor the curriculum to suit the prestige and job expectations of public servants and local NGO personnel, by providing skills and addressing themes of immediate concern to policy-makers and development practitioners. This in turn led Mozambican anthropologists "to critically evaluate canonical expectations of the discipline such as longterm fieldwork, co-research, and forms of public engagement" (Gonçalves, 2019, p. 417).

To account for context, we must always, as students of the human condition, whatever our location, positionality, race, ethnicities, class, social and professional status, gender and sexuality or age, ask ourselves: When and for whom is discipline and conformity needed, desirable, liberating, productive, rational, and an instrument of power and privilege? When and for whom is discipline and conformity needless, undesirable, repressive, unproductive, punishing, irrational, and an instrument of control and delegitimation?

ENDNOTES

1   According to Isaiah Nengo, "the evidence is clear that the origin
    and diversification of the hominin lineage occurred in Africa", and
    that as humans, we share far more in common in our ancestry with
    extant apes that most likely evolved in Africa as well, than our zero
    sum evolutionary ambitions of civilisation and modernisation would
    suggest. As he puts it, "Modern chimpanzees, gorillas, gibbons,
    orangs, and humans are but mere twigs on the family tree after the
    end of this grand flowering over millions of years, first in Africa
    and with later immigrant branches outside of Africa" (Nengo, 2018,
    pp. 3–5; see also Nengo et al., 2017).
2   This was a debate initiated and coordinated by three Duke Univer-
    sity professors, with a broad range of support from other academics
    and research funding organisations (Bates et al., 1993).
3   For a much more detailed discussion of what I understand decoloni-
    sation of and convivial scholarship in the academy to mean, see my
    contribution "Decolonizing the university in Africa" (Nyamnjoh,
    2019).
4   Langaa Research and Publishing Common Initiative Group.
    Retrieved from: www.langaa-rpcig.net/ (10 October 2019)
5   The Fage and Oliver Prize. Retrieved from:
    www.asauk.net/news/awards/prizes/ (19 March 2020)

BIBLIOGRAPHY

Achebe, C. (1974[1964]). *Arrow of God*. Oxford: Heinemann (African Writers Series).

Ake, C. (2012[1979]). "Social science as imperialism". In: H. Lauer & K. Anyidoho (Eds.). *Reclaiming the human sciences and humanities through African perspectives, Volume 1* (pp. 1–104). Accra: Sub-Saharan Publishers.

Akyeampong, E. (2012). "The African voice in African Studies today". In: H. Lauer & K. Anyidoho (Eds.). *Reclaiming the human sciences and humanities through African perspectives, Volume 2* (pp. 982–989). Accra: Sub-Saharan Publishers.

Bates, R. H., Mudimbe, V. Y., & O'Barr Jean (Eds.) (1993). *Africa and the disciplines: The contributions of research in Africa to the social sciences and humanities*. Chicago: University of Chicago Press.

Collyer, F., Connell, R., Maia, J. Ì. L. A., & Morrell, R. (2019). *Knowledge and global power: Making new sciences in the South*. Chicago: University of Chicago Press.

Comaroff J., & Comaroff J. (2010[1991]). "Africa observed: Discourses of the imperial imagination". In: R. R. Grinker, S. C. Lubkemann, & C. B. Steiner (Eds.). *Perspectives on Africa: A reader in culture, history, and representation* (pp. 31–43). Chichester: Wiley-Blackwell.

Comaroff, J., & Comaroff, J. (2011). *Theory from the South: Or how Euro-America is evolving toward Africa*. London: Paradigm.

Connell, R. (2007). *Southern theory: Social science and the global dynamics of knowledge*. Cambridge: Polity.

Cooper B., & Morrell, R. (Eds.) (2014). *Africa-centred knowledges: crossing fields & worlds*. Woodbridge: James Currey.

Devisch R. (2017). *Body and affect in the intercultural encounter*. Bamenda/Leiden: Langaa/African Studies Centre, Leiden.

Emeagwali, G., &. Sefa Dei, G. J. (2014). "Introduction". In: G. Emeagwali & G. J. Sefa Dei (Eds.). *African indigenous knowledge and the disciplines*. Rotterdam: Sense Publishers.

Gonçalves, E. (2019). "African anthropological practice in the 'era of aid': Towards a critique of disciplinary canons". In: R. R. Grinker, S. C. Lubkemann, C. B. Steiner, & E. Gonçalves (Eds.). *A Companion to the anthropology of Africa* (pp. 415–438). Hoboken: Wiley.

Gupta, A., & Ferguson, J. (1992). Beyond 'culture': space, identity, and the politics of difference. *Cultural Anthropology,* 7(1): 6–23.

Gupta, A. & Ferguson, J. (Eds.) (1997). *Anthropological locations: Boundaries and grounds of a field science*. Berkeley: University of California Press.

Harrison, F. V. (1991). "Anthropology as an agent of transformation: Introductory comments and queries". In: F. V. Harrison (Ed.). *Decolonizing anthropology* (pp. 1–14). Washington, D.C.: American Anthropological Association, Association of Black Anthropologists.

Harrison, F. V. (2008). *Outsider within: Reworking anthropology in the global age*. Illinois: University of Illinois Press.

Harrison, F. V. (2012). Dismantling anthropology's domestic and international peripheries. *World Anthropologies Network (WAN) E-Journal*, 6: 87–109.

Harrison, F. V. (2016). Theorizing in ex-centric sites. *Anthropological Theory*, 16(2–3): 160–176.

Harrison, F. V. (2019). "Unraveling race for the twenty-first century". In: J. MacClancy (Ed.). *Exotic no more: Anthropology for the contemporary world* (pp. 77–103). Chicago: Chicago University Press.

Hoffmann, N. (2017). *The knowledge commons, pan-Africanism, and epistemic inequality: A study of CODESRIA* (Doctoral dissertation). Rhodes University, South Africa.

Hountondji, P. (Ed.) (1997). *Endogenous knowledge: Research trails*. Dakar: CODESRIA.

Kuwayama, T. (2017). Japanese anthropology, neoliberal knowledge structuring, and the rise of audit culture: Lessons from the academic world system. *Asian Anthropology*, 16(3): 159–171.

Lategan, B. C. (2018). In praise of strangeness. Exploring the hermeneutical potential of an unlikely source. *Stellenbosch Theological Journal*, 4(1): 267–296.

Morrison, T. (2019). *The source of self-regard: Selected essays, speeches, and meditations*. New York: Alfred A. Knopf.

Nengo, I. (2018). Great ape haters. *Anthropology News*, 59(5): 3–5.

Nengo, I., Tafforeau, P., Gilbert, C. C., Fleagle, J. G., Miller, E. R., Feibel, C., Fox, D. L., Feinberg, J., Pugh, K. D., Berruyer, C., Mana, S., Engle, Z., & Spoor, F. (2017). New infant cranium from the African Miocene sheds light on ape evolution. *Nature*, 548(7666), 169–174. doi:10.1038/nature23456

Ntarangwi, M. (2010). *Reversed gaze: An African ethnography of American anthropology*. Champaign, IL: University of Illinois Press.

Ntarangwi, M. (2019). "African participation in, and perspectives on, the politics of knowledge production in Africanist anthropology". In: R. R. Grinker, S. C. Lubkemann, C. B. Steiner, & E. Gonçalves (Eds.). *A Companion to the anthropology of Africa* (pp. 439–458). Hoboken: Wiley.

Nyamnjoh F. B. (2004). From publish or perish to publish and perish: What 'Africa's 100 best books' tell us about publishing Africa. *Journal of Asian and African Studies*, 39(5): 331–355.

Nyamnjoh, F. B. (2010). *Intimate strangers*. Bamenda: Langaa.

Nyamnjoh, F. B. (2012). Blinded by sight: Divining the future of anthropology in Africa. *Africa Spectrum, 47(2–3): 63–92.

Nyamnjoh, F. B. (2016). *#RhodesMustFall: nibbling at resilient colonialism in South Africa*. Bamenda: Langaa.

Nyamnjoh, F. B. (2017/[2015]). Incompleteness: Frontier Africa and the currency of conviviality. *Journal of Asian and African Studies, 52(3): 253–270.

Nyamnjoh, F. B. (2017). *Drinking from the cosmic gourd: How Amos Tutuola can change our minds*. Bamenda: Langaa.

Nyamnjoh, F. B. (2019). Decolonizing the university in Africa. *The Oxford Research Encyclopedia, Politics*. doi:10.1093/acrefore/9780190228637.013.717

Owusu, M. K. (2012[1978]). "Toward an African critique of African ethnography: The usefulness of the useless". In: H. Lauer & K. Anyidoho (Eds.). *Reclaiming the human sciences and humanities through African perspectives, Volume 1* (pp. 77–104). Accra: Sub-Saharan Publishers.

Phipps, A. (2019). *Decolonising multilingualism: Struggles to decreate*. Bristol: Multilingual Matters.

Ritzer, G. (2019[1992]). *The McDonaldization of society: Into the digital age*. Los Angeles: Sage.

Santos, B. S. (2007). *Another knowledge is possible: Beyond northern epistemologies*. London: Verso.

Simmel, G. (1950). The Stranger. In: K. Wolff (Trans.): *The sociology of Georg Simmel* (pp. 402–408). New York: Free Press, 1950.

Tutuola, A. (1952). *The palm-wine drinkard*. London: Faber and Faber.

Tutuola, A. (1954). *My life in the bush of ghosts*. London: Faber and Faber.

CARL SCHLETTWEIN LECTURES

The distinguished lecture of the Centre for African Studies Basel is held in remembrance of Dr h.c. Carl Schlettwein, who played an important part in the development of African Studies at Basel and in the establishment of the Centre. His moral support was supplemented by the generous and farsighted assistance he gave to these activities. Carl Schlettwein was born in Mecklenburg in 1925 and emigrated to South Africa in 1952. Until 1963 he lived in South West Africa, the former German colony that was then under South African administration. When he married Daniela Gsell he moved to Basel. In 1971 Schlettwein founded the Basler Afrika Bibliographien (BAB) as a library and publishing house in order to allow international institutions to access bibliographic information on South West Africa (Namibia). Accordingly, he published the first national bibliography on this African country. Through these activities the BAB contributed to documenting and researching a nation with a particularly difficult history. Other publications dealt with historical, literary and geo-methodological topics, and included titles on Swiss-African relations. From an individualistic private initiative, the BAB developed into an institution open to the public and became a cornerstone of the Centre for African Studies Basel. As the Namibia Resource Centre—Southern Africa Library the institution is of world-wide importance. The Carl Schlettwein Foundation, which was founded in 1994, runs the BAB and supports students and projects in Namibia as well as in other Southern African countries. In 2001, the Carl Schlettwein Foundation funded the establishment of the Chair of African History, providing the basis for today's professorship in African History and the African Studies programme at the University of Basel. The Foundation works closely with the Centre for African Studies Basel to provide support for teaching and research and in 2016 it enabled the Centre to establish a position on Namibian and Southern African Studies. The University of Basel honoured Carl Schlettwein with an honorary doctorate in 1997.

Printed in the United States
By Bookmasters